Queen Butterfly

by Julie Murray

Abdo Kids Jumbo is an Imprint of Abdo Kids
abdobooks.com

abdobooks.com

Published by Abdo Kids, a division of ABDO, P.O. Box 398166, Minneapolis, Minnesota 55439.

Printed in the United States of America, North Mankato, Minnesota.

102024

012025

THIS BOOK CONTAINS RECYCLED MATERIALS

Photo Credits: Alamy, Animals Animals, Getty Images, Minden Pictures, Shutterstock

Production Contributors: Teddy Borth, Jennie Forsberg, Grace Hansen
Design Contributors: Candice Keimig, Pakou Moua

Library of Congress Control Number: 2024936622

Publisher's Cataloging-in-Publication Data

Names: Murray, Julie, author.

Title: Queen butterfly / by Julie Murray

Description: Minneapolis, Minnesota : Abdo Kids, 2025 | Series: Royal animals | Includes online resources and index.

Identifiers: ISBN 9798384903024 (lib. bdg.) | ISBN 9798384903727 (ebook) | ISBN 9798384904076 (Read-to-me ebook)

Subjects: LCSH: Queen butterfly--Juvenile literature. | Butterflies--Juvenile literature. | Insects--Juvenile literature. | Animal kingdom--Juvenile literature.

Classification: DDC 595.78--dc23

Table of Contents

Queen Butterfly 4

Body 10

Food 14

Defense 16

Baby Queen Butterflies 18

More Facts 22

Glossary 23

Index 24

Abdo Kids Code. 24

Queen Butterfly

The queen butterfly lives in the southern United States, Central America, and South America.

North America
Queen butterfly range
Central America
South America

The queen butterfly mainly lives in warm, open fields. It can also be found in deserts, **pastures**, and along roadsides.

Its royal name comes from its look-alike cousin, the **monarch** butterfly. The two butterflies can be hard to tell apart.

scattered white spots
Queen butterfly
Monarch butterfly

Body

The butterfly's **wingspan** can be up to 3.3 inches (8.4 cm) long. Its wings are orange and brown in color.

The tops of the butterfly's wings are bordered in black and have white markings. The undersides of the wings have black and white veins and white spots.

black
border
black and
white veins

Food

Queen butterflies rely on milkweed as a **host** plant and for **nectar**. They also get nectar from other plants. While feeding, they **pollinate** many kinds of flowers.

Defense

The milkweed plant that the queen butterfly feeds from is toxic to **predators**. Birds and other animals have learned not to eat them!

Baby Queen Butterflies

Females lay their eggs on the leaves and stems of milkweed plants. The eggs hatch into caterpillars. They feed on the milkweed.

Fully grown caterpillar
Egg
Newly hatched caterpillar

Caterpillars then form protective shells around their bodies. They change and grow into butterflies. This process takes about 30 days.

More Facts

- Queen butterflies also closely resemble solider butterflies and viceroy butterflies.
- They travel shorter distances than **monarch** butterflies. They tend to stay in warm places all year long.
- Females lay one egg at a time. But they can lay up to 200 eggs in a day!

Glossary

host – a plant or animal that has something else, called a parasite, living on it. The parasite gets its food and energy from the host.

monarch – a ruler such as a king, queen, or emperor.

nectar – the sweet liquid a plant makes that attracts insects and birds.

pasture – a piece of land on which animals are put to graze.

pollinate – to move or carry pollen to a plant, causing the seeds to be fertilized.

predator – an animal that hunts other animals for food.

wingspan – the distance from the tip of one wing of an animal to the tip of the other.

Index

caterpillars 18, 20

Central America 4

coloring 10

eggs 18

food 14, 16, 18

habitat 6

markings 10, 12

monarch butterfly 8

predators 16

range 4

South America 4

United States 4

wings 10, 12

Abdo Kids ONLINE

FREE! ONLINE MULTIMEDIA RESOURCES

Visit **abdokids.com** to access crafts, games, videos, and more!

Use Abdo Kids code

RQK3024

or scan this QR code!